CELEBRATING THE CITY OF KUALA LUMPUR

Celebrating the City of Kuala Lumpur

Walter the Educator

Silent King Books

SILENT KING BOOKS
SKB

Copyright © 2024 by Walter the Educator

All rights reserved. No part of this book may be reproduced in any manner whatsoever without written permission except in the case of brief quotations embodied in critical articles and reviews.

First Printing, 2024

Disclaimer
This book is a literary work; the story is not about specific persons, locations, situations, and/or circumstances unless mentioned in a historical context. Any resemblance to real persons, locations, situations, and/or circumstances is coincidental. This book is for entertainment and informational purposes only. The author and publisher offer this information without warranties expressed or implied. No matter the grounds, neither the author nor the publisher will be accountable for any losses, injuries, or other damages caused by the reader's use of this book. The use of this book acknowledges an understanding and acceptance of this disclaimer.

Celebrating the City of Kuala Lumpur is a souvenir book that belongs to the Celebrating Cities Book Series by Walter the Educator. Collect them all and more books at WaltertheEducator.com

KUALA LUMPUR

In the heart of Malaysia, a city grand,

Celebrating the City of Kuala Lumpur

Kuala Lumpur, where dreams expand,

Celebrating the City of
Kuala Lumpur

Woven with threads of gold,

Celebrating the City of
Kuala Lumpur

Stories of yesterday and tales yet told.

Celebrating the City of
Kuala Lumpur

Beneath the Petronas Towers' gleaming light,

Celebrating the City of
Kuala Lumpur

A skyline that dazzles both day and night,

Celebrating the City of
Kuala Lumpur

Concrete giants reaching for the stars,

Celebrating the City of
Kuala Lumpur

Reflecting hopes from near and far.

Celebrating the City of
Kuala Lumpur

In bustling streets where cultures blend,

Celebrating the City of
Kuala Lumpur

An urban mosaic without end,

Celebrating the City of
Kuala Lumpur

Malay, Chinese, Indian too,

Celebrating the City of Kuala Lumpur

A melting pot where old meets new.

Celebrating the City of
Kuala Lumpur

Markets hum with vibrant song,

Celebrating the City of
Kuala Lumpur

Pasar Seni, where crowds belong,

Celebrating the City of
Kuala Lumpur

Stalls of spices, silk, and art,

Celebrating the City of
Kuala Lumpur

A sensory feast, a beating heart.

Celebrating the City of
Kuala Lumpur

In Brickfields, the scents of spice,

Celebrating the City of Kuala Lumpur

Curry leaves and jasmine rice,

Celebrating the City of
Kuala Lumpur

Temples rise with vivid hues,

Celebrating the City of
Kuala Lumpur

In Little India, the world renews.

Celebrating the City of
Kuala Lumpur

The ancient steps of Batu Caves,

Celebrating the City of
Kuala Lumpur

A pilgrimage that seekers brave,

Celebrating the City of
Kuala Lumpur

Murugan stands with steadfast grace,

Celebrating the City of
Kuala Lumpur

Guardian of this sacred place.

Celebrating the City of
Kuala Lumpur

Merdeka Square, with flags unfurled,

Celebrating the City of
Kuala Lumpur

Echoes of freedom that changed the world,

Celebrating the City of
Kuala Lumpur

Colonial past and future bright,

Celebrating the City of
Kuala Lumpur

A nation's spirit, pure delight.

Celebrating the City of
Kuala Lumpur

Jalan Alor's food stalls beckon,

Celebrating the City of
Kuala Lumpur

With flavors bold, they quickly reckon,

Celebrating the City of
Kuala Lumpur

Satay skewers and durian's might,

Celebrating the City of
Kuala Lumpur

A culinary journey every night.

Celebrating the City of
Kuala Lumpur

Lush green parks in urban sprawl,

Celebrating the City of
Kuala Lumpur

Lake Gardens where whispers call,

Celebrating the City of
Kuala Lumpur

Orchids bloom, a floral fest,

Celebrating the City of
Kuala Lumpur

In nature's lap, we find our rest.

Celebrating the City of
Kuala Lumpur

May this ode capture your essence true,

Celebrating the City of
Kuala Lumpur

A city where the old meets new,

Celebrating the City of
Kuala Lumpur

Kuala Lumpur, jewel bright,

Celebrating the City of
Kuala Lumpur

A beacon in the velvet night.

Celebrating the City of
Kuala Lumpur

ABOUT THE CREATOR

Walter the Educator is one of the pseudonyms for Walter Anderson. Formally educated in Chemistry, Business, and Education, he is an educator, an author, a diverse entrepreneur, and he is the son of a disabled war veteran. "Walter the Educator" shares his time between educating and creating. He holds interests and owns several creative projects that entertain, enlighten, enhance, and educate, hoping to inspire and motivate you.

Follow, find new works, and stay up to date
with Walter the Educator™
at WaltertheEducator.com

www.ingramcontent.com/pod-product-compliance
Lightning Source LLC
LaVergne TN
LVHW012050070526
838201LV00082B/3899